LIFE'S

a journey

not a destination

How to Live for Each Moment and Find Adventure in Every Day

Vicki Vrint

summersdale

LIFE'S A JOURNEY, NOT A DESTINATION

An Hachette UK Company
www.hachette.co.uk

Summersdale Publishers Ltd
Part of Octopus Publishing Group Limited
Carmelite House
50 Victoria Embankment
LONDON
EC4Y 0DZ
UK

www.summersdale.com

Printed and bound in China

ISBN: 978-1-78783-560-3

Contents

*It is good to have an
end to journey toward;
but it is the journey
that matters, in the end.*

URSULA K. LE GUIN

Introduction

Life's a journey – and what a journey it is! There are twists and turns, detours and delays, high points, a few low points and a wonderful mixture of everyday blessings in between. But when time flies past so quickly, it can be tricky to appreciate the good things, let alone relax and enjoy the activities we love.

The good news is that any one of us can transform an ordinary life into an extraordinary one, and this book shows you how. You don't need a big budget or hours of free time to succeed – in fact, you can start right now by rediscovering the magic in everyday moments. A few simple changes to your routine will bring extra joy to your day, too, and as you progress through the book you'll free up the time – and build up the confidence – to go for your bigger goals and dreams.

From simple tips to exciting challenges, from questionnaires to inspirational quotes, this book will help you to make each day special and fall in love with life again.

START WHERE
you are

The adventure starts here, with you finding the hidden moments of joy that are already scattered throughout your day, and adding in more where you can. There are so many things you can do right away to make your life more exciting and fulfilling, from simple changes like freshening up your routines or focusing on the little things that make you smile, to learning how to change your mindset and see the world in a different light. In this chapter you'll get the chance to identify the things you love, and to discover ways to make sure that every day includes something special.

Press pause
and breathe

The first skill you need to transform your life is also the simplest – to learn to press pause and take a minute or two to focus on your breathing. By doing this, you'll be training yourself to be present in the moment, rather than rushing through your day on "autopilot" and missing out on the little things that make life wonderful. This book is full of ideas to help you reconnect with these special moments, but for now training yourself to take "breathing breaks" is a great start. Make them a regular event by taking one every time you boil the kettle or looking out of the window and watching the world go by: simply step away from your tasks, breathe and tune in to your feelings.

Live
and love

EACH MOMENT

Better break times

If it feels like you just can't fit any "me time" into your current routine, think again. You can get a great boost from the smallest moments. Hopefully you already have at least ten minutes to yourself to relax at some point in the day, so start by making these existing breaks extra special.

Ensure you have somewhere clutter-free and calm to enjoy your downtime. At home, have a cosy corner to relax in for ten minutes' peace. If you're at work, try to find a quiet space away from your workstation for your break, sitting outside when you can. Don't check your messages or to-do list; you could read, doodle, meditate or daydream – anything that brings you peace. You'll feel all the better for a proper session of time-out.

Live for
TODAY

Time is precious – *today* is precious – so what are you going to do to make it special? Greet the day with a smile, look forward to the good bits and don't dwell on any tricky moments. Wear your best clothes today: the new top you've been saving or the shoes that are still pristine in their box. Book tickets to the film you've been waiting to see, text the friend you've been meaning to catch up with and, if you can fit in a trip to that park you've never visited before, well, do that too! Seize the day, live for the moment and don't put your happiness on hold.

Gather your gratitude

It's exciting to plan new adventures, but don't forget that there are wonderful moments to be found in your life already. Every evening, sit quietly and think back over your day, reflecting on all the positive moments: the times when things went well or when someone made you laugh or surprised you. Think about any beautiful images or scenes you saw too. Make a note of these gems that brightened your day or simply enjoy reliving them and feeling grateful for your blessings.

What makes you happy?

Working out what makes you happy is important when building your extraordinary life. Use these pages to remind yourself of the things that mean the most to you.

What must you have in your life to be happy? What do you need to feel fulfilled, relaxed or full of joy? If you're not sure, make a note of your happiest moments over the next few days and think about what caused them. It might be spending time outdoors, your daily swim, studying for an evening class, relaxing at home...

I feel happiest when I'm:

_____

_____

_____

_____

_____

_____

_____

_____

_____

When you look back at your choices, you might find you're able to group them together under headings like fitness, creative pursuits, learning, socializing, spiritual moments, etc. Make a note of these areas too.

These types of activity are most important to me:

_____

_____

_____

_____

_____

_____

_____

_____

_____

Now, have a think and see if you can work out how to include more of these activities in your week. If you love exercise, could you make running or cycling a part of your daily travels? If learning is important to you, could you listen to a podcast or use a language app in your lunch break?

I could fit in my favourite activities by:

_____

_____

_____

_____

_____

_____

_____

Don't worry if you can't think of ways to include all your favourite things just now. We'll look at tips for making more time in your schedule later in this chapter.

Clear out the clutter

In many ways, clutter is a sign of the past crowding in on us: it takes up our time, fills up our homes and stops us from enjoying the present. Clear the decks and declutter your house, and you'll be giving yourself the time and space to enjoy the things that really matter.

If a clean-up operation seems like a huge task, start small with an area that always catches your eye and you're sure to feel inspired by the results. You'll also feel calmer, lighter, happier and less stressed – decluttering really can have life-changing effects. When you've cleared a room, don't be afraid to move furniture around or shake things up a bit to give your space a fresh, new feel.

Let today
be the
start of
something new

One can choose to go
back toward safety or
forward toward growth.

Abraham Maslow

SORT OUT
your schedule

If you take a look at how you currently spend your time, you're sure to find ways you can improve your schedule and fit in more of the activities you love. So grab a pencil and paper and take an honest look at what you do with your waking hours.

Start by asking yourself some basic questions:

- Is your current schedule working for you?

- Are there moments that you dread, when you feel particularly rushed or stressed?

- Would you like more time for family or hobbies?

Next, draw out a timetable of your week and fill in all your activities so you can see how your time is spent. (You could even colour code different categories, such as work, leisure, meal times, travel, time wasted, etc.) Now, try the following:

1. Identify the tasks you really dislike: how can you improve these? Can you delegate them, do them more efficiently or drop them altogether? Be ruthless – your quality of life is important!

2. Pinpoint any wasted moments, such as those spent sitting in traffic or browsing online. These can really add up. How can you make the time more useful or joyful? Could you listen to a meditation, watch an inspirational talk or plan your next big adventure instead?

3. Look back at your list of things that make you happy. Can you spot ways you could include more of these activities in your week?

Now re-draw your timetable including any improvements you've made. Schedule any study activities for times when you're at your brightest, and aim to include at least two moments of "me time" a day – one for meditation or relaxation, and one to do something that makes you happy. Try to include a longer session of time to catch up with friends once a week too.

MONEY
matters

It may not be the most fun task, but taking stock of your finances is crucial if you're going to plan adventures, big or small. There are plenty of apps to help you. Remind yourself that you work hard for your money, and make sure that every penny you spend goes toward something worthwhile that you will use or enjoy.

Money worries can also be a cause of stress, but if you sort out your financial troubles you'll be able to relax fully and enjoy the exciting new experiences you've got in store.

Go through your current outgoings carefully and be realistic about which things you actually need. Cut out any unused subscriptions and shop around for cheaper options when you're choosing household services – remember that suppliers will take advantage of you if you don't do this. It's also worth taking note of how the little "treats" (such as daily coffees or snacks) can add up.

Your finances shouldn't stop you from pursuing your dreams, so if you've got a goal in mind, go for it! You'll be surprised at the savings you can make if you try. Learn to economize, cut back on the treats and put the money towards achieving your ambition instead.

You
CHOOSE

You are in control of your life – you really are! It may feel as though you're at the mercy of your responsibilities and don't have any freedom to follow your heart, but realizing that *you* are ultimately in the driving seat can be a real game-changer.

Every day you're faced with dozens of small decisions – the route you take to work, the opportunities you're offered, the responsibilities you take on, the way you respond to good or bad news – and with every one of these choices you have the power to change your situation in some way. So, think carefully about each choice you make and own your decisions, and pick the most interesting path wherever possible.

Every choice you make can CHANGE YOUR LIFE

Check your connections

The relationships you have with those around you will have a huge impact on your everyday life, so give your interactions with others some thought and spend time with positive, upbeat people whenever you can. Avoid those who lower your mood or spread negativity, if possible, and sort out any unresolved issues you have with others so that you can move on. By improving your current relationships you'll not only experience more happiness every day, but you'll be laying good foundations for the new connections you'll make when you meet people on your journey.

Decide what matters most

There's one more area to explore to help you live an extraordinary life: your values. We don't often set aside time to think about this, but once you've identified your priorities you'll be able to make sure you focus on them when making any big decisions. Take a look at these questions to help you consider what matters most to you.

The people I admire most are:

_____

_____

_____

_____

The qualities they have are:

_____

_____

_____

_____

Now identify the top five values that are important to you. You can use the word cloud below for further ideas.

AMBITION   Balance   INTELLIGENCE

Kindness   Appreciation   Honesty

Courage   Love

Encouragement   Loyalty   Positivity

My five core values are:

1. _____
2. _____
3. _____
4. _____
5. _____

Your list may include values you already live by as well as those you want to cultivate more. You could brainstorm each one, then think about whether your current roles in life allow you to honour them. How could you change things, if they don't?

You might find it useful to write a "personal statement" that summarizes the values you identified. For example, "I'm a thoughtful and positive person who values authenticity and practises kindness and compassion every day." You could repeat this as a daily affirmation, if you like.

My personal statement:

_____
_____
_____
_____
_____
_____

Life should not just *be lived;* IT SHOULD BE CELEBRATED

Don't put it off

Putting off tedious tasks may seem like a good choice at the time, but there's nothing worse than having those stubborn unticked chores hanging around at the bottom of your to-do list. They'll prey on your mind, stop you from enjoying your time out and – even worse – they'll hold you back from pursuing new goals.

Become a doer, not a delayer, and practise proactivity. If a job needs sorting, do it today – or at least take the first step. If a job takes less than five minutes, do it *now*. You'll end up feeling super-efficient, relieved and inspired all at once!

Action
always
BEATS
INTENTION

Don't let the fear of falling
keep you from climbing up.

Constance Chuks Friday

Positivity training

Adopting a positive rather than a negative attitude to your day, your self and life in general will transform the way you experience things, and gear you up to go for your dreams as well. Preparing for the worst-case scenario is a habit that may have kept our ancestors safe thousands of years ago, but visualizing positive outcomes is the way ahead for you now. Use this page to surround yourself with mood-boosting words and thoughts – there's space for you to jot down your own ideas too.

Next time you hear yourself using negative words, try some of these positive alternatives instead:

Negative word	Positive word
Failure	Lesson
Nervous	Excited
Problem	Challenge
Boring	Dependable
I hate	I prefer
I'm being stupid	I'm working on understanding this
I should be	I'm choosing to
I can't	Instead I can try

Turn negative situations into positive ones

Practise finding a positive in everyday problems and you'll train your brain to look on the bright side and experience more happiness.

Situation:	Positives:
e.g. you took a wrong turn on your route	e.g. you spotted a great restaurant to try out

TAKING THE
first steps

You've made a great start by looking at where you are at the moment – now it's time to think about where you're heading and take a few steps in the right direction. This chapter shows you that small changes make a difference and it challenges you to take a trip to the edge of your comfort zone. There are tips on goal-setting and the practicalities of prioritizing, but – don't worry – there are plenty of easy ideas for adding excitement to your day too.

In fact, if you've ever wondered how to make housework fun, this is definitely the chapter for you!

Practise purposeful living

Start each day with the intention to do something that makes a difference – however small – to your own life or someone else's, and then go ahead and do it. When you wake up, decide on your worthwhile activity and write it down if you like. Make sure it's something that inspires you to leap out of bed, not to hide under the sheets! *Today I'm going to pay someone a compliment... pick up some litter... plan my dream road-trip... declutter and donate some clothes to charity...* Your sense of purpose will motivate you and you'll get a great sense of satisfaction from achieving your goal.

*The meaning of life
is to find your gift.
The purpose of life
is to give it away.*

PABLO PICASSO

BE
childlike

Think back to how exciting life was when you were a child – how every day was full of adventure and you were prepared to come up with some pretty good staying-up-late strategies so that it didn't have to end. What's changed? Well, you have!

As we grow older we lose many of the things that make life more fun: a spirit of adventure; a sense of wonder at the world around us; our imagination; the knowledge that play is important; dirty knees; the belief that we can do anything we want with our lives; the desire to write poems or paint... and why did we all stop dressing up?! Well, don't worry – all of these things are still possible. It's time to tune in to your inner child.

Here are some activities to lose yourself in, and they're a great reminder that you don't need to spend money to add fun to your day. Look back at your childhood photos for more inspiration – your favourite hobbies are just waiting to be rediscovered.

Retro books and computer games — revisit some classics.

Play games — board games, card games, word games and puzzles have no significance in the great scheme of things but are simply fun to do.

Play with your food — bake and decorate gingerbread people, invent an epic new sandwich.

Go to an adventure playground — it's empty all day when the kids are at school.

Wonder at nature — look for bugs with a magnifying glass or find shapes in the clouds; splash in puddles or gather materials for a natural collage.

Dress up — organize a fancy-dress party or go to a convention dressed as your favourite character.

Run for fun — put on your sports gear but forget your training app. Just sprint across the park at top speed to feel the wind in your face, or hurtle down a hill.

Draw, paint, colour... model your friends and family out of salt dough to unwind! Try some finger-painting and get really messy.

Savour excitement

Getting excited about an upcoming event is often as much a part of the enjoyment as the activity itself. The anticipation will lift your spirits and carry you through mundane moments. It's wonderful to have a big treat on the horizon, but once you start to tune in to smaller blessings, you'll be able to find something to look forward to every day.

Each morning, pick a treat to enjoy later in the day and savour the anticipation as the moment approaches. Your treat doesn't need to be anything extravagant – a quick break to read your favourite book or to listen to some music can be more rewarding than buying yourself a coffee and a cake. (Although combining all of those things would be lovely too!)

Make it fun!

We all have to do tasks that are a bit of a drag, but there's usually something you can do to make even the most repetitive of chores a little more fun. If you have to spend half an hour cleaning the car, for example, why not put on your favourite playlist and have a soundtrack to get you moving? Or you could group together any easy indoor tasks – such as ironing, dusting and polishing shoes – and put on an episode of your favourite TV series while you do them. You could fit in some fitness by making the vacuuming part of a workout, use the washing-up as a moment to mindfully focus on the sensations around you, or set yourself a time challenge when changing the sheets or hanging up the laundry.

My joyful day

With a little thought, you can add something positive to almost every part of your day, so get creative and use this page to brainstorm some ideas for turning a mundane Monday (or Tuesday... or Wednesday...) into something worth jumping out of bed for.

Wake up	e.g. try some yoga stretches, set a positive intention for the day
Shower/getting ready	e.g. create a morning playlist to boost your mood
Breakfast	e.g. eat mindfully, treat yourself to a special breakfast, catch up with family (no phones allowed!)
Commute	e.g. try a new route to work, fit in some exercise
Work	e.g. share some snacks, brighten up your work area
Lunch break	e.g. add in a walk, eat somewhere new, do a guided meditation
After work	e.g. visit somewhere new on your journey home, travel with a friend
Chores	e.g. set a timer, get them done and make them fun
Leisure time	e.g. enjoy a treat that you've been anticipating all day
Bedtime	e.g. unwind with journaling, have a luxurious bath, develop a bedtime ritual

Change the way you look at things
and the things you look at change.

Wayne Dyer

SAY YES / SAY NO

Now that you've worked out what's important to you in life, it's time to start putting that knowledge into practice as you choose what to do each day. This means learning when to say yes and when to say no. Your life will feel more fulfilled if you say yes to the things that matter, and no to the things you'd rather avoid. Life is never quite that simple, of course, but it *is* important to say no to extra responsibilities that you don't have time for in a polite but firm way. So your first challenge is:

Say no to something you'd rather not take on

... and free up some extra time to spend with family or on your favourite hobby.

Saying yes to things can be tricky too. Perhaps you've been invited to try out an activity with a group of friends or offered a new responsibility at work. You'd really like to give it a go, but you're worried that you won't be up to the challenge. The only sure-fire way you'll fail is if you don't give it a try, so don't let your fears hold you back. There are wonderful experiences waiting just outside your comfort zone – and even if you don't get things right first time, there are lessons to be learnt and laughs to be had, so your next challenge is to:

Say yes to something you'd love to try

Your new "I can do it" attitude will help you invite in lots of new experiences.

Life's an
adventure,
SO LIVE IT
THAT WAY

GOAL
setting

Every journey needs direction – and setting goals is a brilliant way to inspire you and motivate you to take action. Now you've cleared some space in your schedule to pursue your dreams and thought about the things you'd like to work towards, use the following pages to set yourself some goals. Then you just need to tune in to your enthusiasm and start your quest!

1. You must **enjoy the process** of working towards your goal to stay motivated and happy, so don't plan a novel if you hate writing! The steps you take every day towards achieving your dream should be as much fun as the end result.

2. If you've set a long-term goal, **be flexible.** You might decide to take a different direction once you get started – and that's great! It's fine to move the goalposts.

When you're setting your goals it might help to look back at pages 28–29 to remind yourself of the values that are important to you. If you're not enjoying your work, for example, perhaps it's because it's not creative enough, and you really value creativity. Changing your job is one option – and could be your long-term goal – but you might want to pick a more manageable step to begin with. Perhaps you could find ways to add some creativity into your current job or try some voluntary work in a more appealing area first? Or you could find a creative outlet in a hobby or evening class instead.

My goals

This table will help you take a look at the different areas of your life and think about any goals you might like to set. The column on the right is for you to plan your first move – it's great to have a practical plan in place, and taking that initial step in the right direction is a brilliant feeling too. If you can, schedule in a little time each week to work towards your dreams.

AREA	How do you feel about this area of your life? ☺ / ☺ / ☹	What would you like to change?
Work		
Physical health		
Emotional well-being		
Family		
Home		
Hobbies		
Relationships		
Causes that matter to me		
Creative		
Any others (e.g. spiritual)		

What goal would you like to set?	What's the first step you can take?

Change one Thing

Small changes to your routine and lifestyle add up, so if want to work on an area of your life, start by improving just one thing. Perhaps you feel that you need to sort out your diet? Regularly swapping one snack for something healthier is a brilliant way to begin. Or maybe you want to have more time to devote to study – well, getting up just 15 minutes earlier a day will give you almost two hours every week towards your cause. Small changes like these are easier to fit in and stick to, so change one little thing today and look forward to big results.

Learn to experiment

We are creatures of habit, but by always taking the same route to work, eating in the same cafe or rewatching a favourite box set, we're missing out on the chance to discover something new and exciting. This book is full of ideas for fitting new experiences into your life, but start now with something small and you'll see how easy and rewarding it can be to freshen up your day. You could try wearing something different, listening to a new type of music or taking an unusual route to work. You'll find yourself noticing the details of your new experience, rather than drifting through it.

Every small step is a step in the right direction

Lose The Labels

Many of us are sensitive to other people's views about us, but there's no need to accept them – especially if they're limiting ones! Perhaps you were always told that no one in your family was sporty or artistic and so you've never given these activities a try? But with so many options out there – from martial arts to athletics and playing the guitar to pottery – there's sure to be something that you've got a real talent for.

We can be guilty of labelling ourselves too, thinking we must be shy if we've ever felt anxious in an intimidating situation, for example. But our emotions are fleeting reactions to the moment and don't need to be carried with us. Resolve to live a label-free life; to take each challenge as it comes; and to try out something you've always shied away from. Don't leave your strengths undiscovered – you could be missing out on some brilliant opportunities.

The greatest danger
in life is not taking
the adventure.

Brian Blessed

If at first you DON'T SUCCEED...

For many of us the idea of getting things wrong is a negative one. School taught us to aim for ticks rather than crosses on our homework, and as adults we can end up with a fear of failure, which may stop us from trying out new experiences. But no one gets perfect results every time – life's just not like that – so next time things don't go according to plan, remind yourself that we can learn our best lessons from our mistakes.

Once you discover that it's not the end of the world if you mess up, you'll feel less stressed and much more confident about embracing life's opportunities... and that can only lead to more fun and excitement.

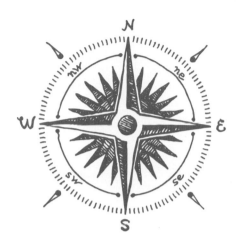

*Every child is an
artist, until he's told
he's not an artist.*

JOHN LENNON

Celebrate small wins

There's so much to celebrate in day-to-day life if we stop to think about it... and find time for a little celebration! Whether it's an achievement at work, a change in the weather or your sports team winning a match, mark the occasion with a treat: a cheerful message to a friend or a mini get-together (any excuse for a coffee!). When you start acknowledging the small wins, you'll realize just how many of them there are. (Don't forget to celebrate the small steps you take when you're working towards your goals – this will keep you inspired and help you to enjoy your projects even more.)

Walk
your
path
WITH
CONFIDENCE

LIVING IN
the moment

Your day is made up of many little moments and this chapter shows you how to make the most of them. Mindfulness is the perfect antidote to rushing through your day on autopilot, and here you'll discover simple ways to live mindfully, to slow down and to appreciate the present. You'll also learn how to make every moment count by enjoying the good things around you and adding some spontaneous fun to your week.

Making it
mindful

Mindfulness is about finding a way to anchor yourself in the present so that you can become aware of your thoughts, feelings and surroundings. You can do almost anything in a mindful way – you just need to remind yourself to stop and tune in to your senses. If you're new to the idea, you could start by picking a daily task and doing it mindfully. You could take a mindful shower, for example, focusing on the sound of the running water and the warmth of it on your skin.

Mindfulness also gives us a chance to observe our thoughts, by practising "being". You could try this by simply sitting still, focusing on the sensations around you and letting your thoughts come and go. There's no need to try to clear your mind, just note your thoughts and let them pass without judging them in any way.

Inhabit
the moment,
and LET YOUR
JUDGEMENTS GO

My mindful moments

Make a note of your mindful experiences here.

Mindful moment

Date: ....

Where I was: ....

What I was doing: ....

What I could see/hear/sense: ....

How I felt: ....

My thoughts: ....

Mindful moment

Date: ....

Where I was: ....

What I was doing: ....

What I could see/hear/sense: ....

How I felt: ....

My thoughts: ....

Mindful moment

Date: ....

Where I was: ....

What I was doing: ....

What I could see/hear/sense: ....

How I felt: ....

My thoughts: ....

Mindful moment

Date: ....

Where I was: ....

What I was doing: ....

What I could see/hear/sense: ....

How I felt: ....

My thoughts: ....

REFLECTING

If you don't already include a moment or two for meditation in your day, now is a good time to start. Taking time out to quieten your mind will have a really beneficial impact on your emotional well-being and is a great way to combat stress. Meditation has even been shown to change your neural pathways – so you can actually rewire your brain by taking a few minutes every day to try this relaxing practice.

Don't be put off if you've never given it a go before or if the thought of sitting silently is a little intimidating. You could always try listening to a guided meditation. There are some brilliant apps to help you get started and the more often you practise the more you'll benefit.

Journaling

If meditation doesn't appeal to you, you could try journaling for five minutes every evening. This is another really simple practice that allows your brain to process everything you've experienced in the day, and it can be a great de-stressor too. All you need is a notebook and pen (or a laptop or writing app, if you prefer).

Settle down quietly at the end of the day and write about anything you like. You could record your favourite moments – or offload the stressiest ones! You could use the time to write about your goals and ambitions, your feelings or your worries. If you prefer a more structured approach there are plenty of themed journals available with writing cues to get you started.

A photo challenge

Most of us don't get the chance to appreciate the details of our surroundings – if we're out and about, we've usually got a destination in mind and a time limit to get there. A lovely way to help you slow down and notice the little things is to challenge yourself to take interesting photos of your surroundings when you're on a journey. Try to avoid an obvious picture and go for something unusual instead. You could focus on the details of a building; look for a quirky way to frame a shot; take a picture at a different angle or compose one in black and white. When you start to see the familiar in a new way, you appreciate everything around you so much more.

Pick a
MOOD-BOOSTER

Next time you have ten minutes to yourself, add some fun to your day with one of these speedy mood-boosters. (I'm sure you can think of others to add to the list too.) If you can't decide which to pick, why not roll a die and enjoy the corresponding burst of random fun from the list below.

1. Go outside and enjoy ten minutes of fresh air – whatever the weather!

2. Recharge with a drink, snack, book, or tech-based treat of your choice.

3. Laugh – at a clip of your favourite comedy show, watch a YouTube compilation, or ask a friend to tell you a joke.

4. Listen to some music – it boosts your mood and, if you dance along, it will boost your heart-rate too.

5. Make someone smile – for an instant release of happy hormones and to spread some good cheer.

6. Enjoy a chat with a friend.

Seize the day, don't wish it away

Turn things you've
always wanted to do
into things you've done.

T. S. Eliot

BECOME
an explorer

Life is a journey that offers you wonderful surprises and detours on the way – you just have to develop an explorer's mindset and be prepared to give them a try. A good way to practise this is by being spontaneous and going "off plan" when you're out and about. If you're on your usual lunchtime walk around the block, for example, and you see a sign for an exhibition, craft sale or nature trail, why not investigate that instead? Taking a new route to work or using a different mode of transport can reveal other areas for you to explore or activities to try out when you can.

If you've got more time on your hands get hold of a detailed map (or app) and rediscover the area around your home: follow footpaths, climb hills and look for ancient ruins. Or visit somewhere completely new for no reason other than to explore. Who knows what you'll discover?

Being adventurous like this can help you to be spontaneous in other areas of your life too. Look out for little opportunities to add some spontaneity to your day and say yes to experiences you might normally turn down. Invite excitement in by looking out for life's detours and you're sure to have fun.

Switch up your treats

→

Make sure you appreciate any little luxuries you treat yourself to each month by choosing carefully and picking something you'll have time to enjoy. If you're currently paying for a few different subscriptions every month but not getting the most out of them, think about cancelling and opting for pay-as-you-go passes, as and when you use them. Monthly fees for the gym and cinema or TV and music services, plus other treats such as magazine or food subscriptions, can be expensive, so you'll free up some money to put towards your savings goals.

Ten-minute task bursts

We are all guilty of putting off projects that seem too overwhelming to start. We might tell ourselves that we need a couple of hours to complete them and then somehow never find the time. There's no need to miss out on achieving things when there are moments in your day you can use towards reaching your goals.

Almost every task can be broken down into smaller steps, whether you're planning a road trip or applying for a new job, so schedule in a ten-minute task burst whenever suits you best – early morning, in your lunch break, or after you've eaten your evening meal – and use the time to focus completely on your project. You'll be surprised at how much you can achieve in ten minutes a day.

"One day" or "day one"

— YOU DECIDE

INDULGE
yourself

It's simple to add little indulgences to your week. They'll not only give you a sense of fulfilment, but they'll be mindful experiences too as you're treating your senses – a double boost for your emotional well-being! Why not try:

A luxury bath with scented candles, music, your favourite bath products and some soft towels on standby.

Bake yourself a treat – fill your kitchen with the aroma of baking and make your favourite cake or dessert.

Cocoon yourself in a cosy corner with blankets, cushions and a comforting hot drink.

Try out some simple self-massage and check out the acupressure points on your hands and feet. Use a little of your favourite essential oil for a relaxing treatment.

Nurture mind, body and spirit with a walk outside in the most natural environment you can find. Focus on the wonders around you from clouds, trees and fields to the creatures you encounter there.

Mindful treat times

Keep a record of your most indulgent mindful moments and revisit them whenever you like.

Date:

_____

Treat:

_____

Where I went:

_____

_____

What I did:

_____

_____

Which senses I indulged:

☐ Sight ☐ Sound ☐ Touch ☐ Taste ☐ Smell

How I felt:

_____

_____

_____

_____

_____

Date:
_____

Treat:
_____

Where I went:
_____
_____

What I did:
_____
_____

Which senses I indulged:

☐ Sight ☐ Sound ☐ Touch ☐ Taste ☐ Smell

How I felt:
_____
_____
_____
_____
_____

Make it musical

Music is a powerful way to transform your experiences and boost your mood. You can add a soundtrack to almost any part of your day, whether it's instrumental music while you're working, something inspirational to liven up your daily commute, or dancing-round-doing-the-cleaning music to speed you through the housework. Music can help you relax or meditate or transport you off to your own little haven for a song or two. If you can play an instrument, that's even better – and even if you can't, *everyone* can sing in their own unique way, so fit in a five-minute burst of music-making once a day to help you relax.

Giving

Carrying out an act of kindness will spread a little happiness and make your day feel rather wonderful. (In fact, studies have shown that acts of generosity bring great benefits to the person who carries them out, as well as to the recipients.) There are so many ways you can put a smile on someone else's face, so try out some of these suggestions or get creative and come up with some of your own:

- Pay for a suspended coffee

- Leave a book in a public place with a note on for someone else to enjoy

- Pay someone a compliment

- Chalk a positive message on the pavement

- Share something uplifting or kind on social media

- Tell a friend how much they mean to you

- Leave a sticky note with a joke on for a stranger to find

- Volunteer for a local cause

Every day,
let your

soul sing

To finish the moment, to find the journey's end in every step of the road, to live the greatest number of good hours, is wisdom.

Ralph Waldo Emerson

Mindful
RELATIONSHIPS

Bringing mindfulness to your interactions will have a really positive effect on your relationships and transform your day. Whether you're chatting to a friend or talking to a colleague about work, practise mindful listening, focusing on what the other person is saying, rather than letting your attention waver or thinking up a reply. When you do answer, try to be positive and understanding, and show that you've listened to their point of view. Try to look for the good in people, spreading kindness and encouragement when you can. And treat yourself to at least one focused, thoughtful or funny conversation with someone you care about every day.

Listen.
Understand.
Connect.
LOVE.

FINDING
adventure

Congratulations! You're ready for bigger challenges and even more exciting quests, and this chapter is here to inspire you, whether you want to plan an epic expedition or enjoy a short, sharp adrenaline hit. But adventures don't have to involve extreme sports or long trips – there are plenty of challenging things you can try at home too, from learning a language to changing someone else's life, and from beating your phobias to building a bucket list. So strap in and get ready as you speed away from your comfort zone and head for the horizon!

Get learning

Most of us would love to learn something new, whether it's a language, a sport or how to fly a plane, and there are plenty of benefits to be had from the process, besides enjoying your new-found ability. Learning boosts your brain power, self-esteem and mental health – as well as your prospects – and you'll get the social benefits of studying with others too.

Search around for a good teacher, group or app to kick-start your project and don't forget that you can find some great free resources at your library or online. It's fun to record your progress in your journal, but remember to focus on enjoying your day-to-day achievements – it's not all about the end goal. If you're not sure which new skill to pick, why not give a few a try and see what suits you: there's so much to learn out there, you're sure to find something you'll love and excel at.

What we learn
with pleasure we
never forget.

ALFRED MERCIER

Join a Team

If you haven't played a team sport since school, how about taking to the court (or pitch) and giving your favourite game another go? There are plenty of options to choose from, such as joining a football or netball squad, or playing doubles at tennis or badminton. Being part of a team will help you to hone your abilities, appreciate your strengths, work with others and speak up for yourself too. You'll get the benefits of regular exercise and a wonderful, mood-boosting feeling of belonging... plus there are the post-match celebrations to look forward to, of course! If sport isn't really your thing, there are other team activities to tempt you – perhaps you could join a quiz team, debating group or choir.

Two-week
TRY OUT

It's time to focus on one of those things you've "always been meaning to try" and – finally – give it a go. Perhaps you've decluttered your schedule but still not found the time to build an art portfolio, transform your fitness regime or learn to ride a motorbike... well if you really want to follow your dream, you're going to have to do something a bit more drastic and *make* some time.

One option is to take some time off work to concentrate on your goal. Another idea is to make an extra hour in your day – every day – by getting up early for a week or two (rearranging your day a little if necessary) to find the time. Even if you can't complete the whole project in your fortnight of extra hours, at least you'll have made a start and will know whether it's something you'd like to pursue long term.

Do what
you love and

LOVE WHAT

YOU DO

Retreat!

A rewarding way to appreciate everything we take for granted in our day-to-day life is to leave it behind for a little while. You can do this in the simplest of ways: by having a couple of days where you just eat wholesome, nutritious foods, or by taking some digital-downtime and turning off your devices for a while.

But if you want to take things further – and you have the cash to do it – you could go on a retreat and leave the outside world behind for a week or so, or try out a boot camp with an intense exercise programme. You'll appreciate the luxuries and little things you missed so much more when they're reintroduced.

Life is
so much
brighter
when we
FOCUS ON
WHAT MATTERS

One's destination is never
a place, but rather a new
way of looking at things.

Henry Miller

MAKE A
difference

We've talked about how doing something worthwhile will give you a greater sense of worth and boost your day (see page 96), but if you've already made a habit of giving – and cleared some time in your schedule – you may want to take your contributions a step further. Check back to the exercise on pages 28–29 where you identified your values and see if you can think of any areas where you could put your principles into practice and make a difference in a bigger way. Could you mentor someone or sponsor them? Or become an eco-activist? Or donate blood? Would you like to volunteer abroad in an orphanage or animal sanctuary, or do something similar closer to home?

Think about your strengths and how you could use these to support a cause you believe in. If you're really clued up on your subject you might want to write articles or a blog to bring in supporters. If you're a brilliant people person, how about organizing a fundraiser or action group?

There's always a chance to put your skills to use if you think hard enough. Making a positive difference to the world around you is one of the most powerful ways to turn an ordinary life into something extraordinary, so get thinking and see what you can do to change the world.

Get back to nature

Spending time in a natural environment is important for your well-being, and – hopefully – you've already found a few moments in your day to get some fresh air outdoors. (A walk during your lunch break is a great start.) But the more you immerse yourself in the natural world, the better the benefits, so why not try a *really* wild experience?

There are hundreds of different organized wildlife encounters, trips and safaris to choose from online, but it's brilliant fun to simply pick a warm night, pack a sleeping bag and camp out under the stars. There's nothing more magical than hearing the dawn chorus and watching the sun rise. So why not spend a night camping somewhere close to home so that you can watch the changing scenery and experience a different side to your local area.

ADD
adrenaline bursts

Enjoying short intense bursts of excitement will really get your heart pumping. Activities that give you a quick rush of adrenaline are fun – obviously! – and will give you a great sense of achievement, but an adrenaline burst can also help you to release tension and breathe more easily, and heighten your awareness too.

There are dozens of things you can try, from obvious options – such as bungee jumping or parachuting – to more unusual activities like paramotoring (paragliding with a propeller strapped to your back). In many cities you can take in the view from a tall building, but abseiling down it, or stepping out onto a glass-floored observation deck at the top, will *really* get your heart pumping.

Extreme sports and death-defying drops aren't the only adrenaline boosters out there. There are other ways you can get your danger-fix... without spending too much money. You could ask for a race-circuit driving experience for a birthday present, or try driving a tank or tractor instead. Clay-pigeon shooting – and even Viking axe throwing! – are options too, or just challenge yourself to do something that's a little outside your comfort zone. Perhaps you could give a presentation at work, offer the toast at a party or settle down for a night in with a horror movie. You'll enjoy the buzz of completing your challenge and it may even inspire you to seek out another exciting moment or two.

Focus on the extraordinary

Sometimes we can forget that there are so many examples of extraordinary things around us. We might take the community around us for granted, or never stop to hear the stories of the inspirational people we meet. Seek out something incredible every day and take a moment to appreciate just how amazing everyday life can be.

You could start your morning with a surprising nature fact or video clip when you first go online, for example, or read up on the achievements of explorers, scientists or other pioneers. You'll discover some fascinating stories. Don't forget that inspiration can come from people around you too – and not just the ones you hear about in the news. You'll add a little magic to your day when you seek out and celebrate the extraordinary.

Conquer
YOUR FEARS

Everyone has a phobia or two, but facing up to a fear can be character-building and beneficial in lots of ways. You'll also learn that you can beat perceived limitations and change the way you react to things.

It's an empowering and liberating experience: you have to let go and feel your fear, to teach yourself that it isn't a threat after all. Search online for phobia-beating tips and courses, but don't worry if you're not ready to encounter a room full of rattlesnakes or fly in an aeroplane just yet. You can always start with something that's just outside your comfort zone and tackle that first.

Beyond
fear lies
FREEDOM

Energy rightly applied
and directed will
accomplish anything.

Nellie Bly

PLAN A BIG
adventure

Now you've developed an explorer's attitude (see pages 84–85) you're all set to travel farther afield and plan a bigger adventure. The world's an amazing place, full of breath-taking scenery, wonderful wildlife, awesome architecture and incredible people... so get out there and fully embrace it.

Perhaps you already have a dream journey in mind – an Amazon river cruise, a dog-sled trip to see the Northern Lights or a wildlife safari in Africa. If you're not sure, the internet's the place to check out top bucket list destinations, so start with some research and – if you're feeling creative – put together a mood board or Pinterest collection of ideas to get you inspired. Check out any films or novels set in your dream destination too. Once you've chosen a destination, read up on other adventurers' experiences to fill you with enthusiasm and help you plan.

You don't need to travel to the other side of the world to enjoy an adventure, but try to take in a different destination and enjoy a change of culture if you can. Planning your trip should be part of the fun. Set up a savings account and budget for your expedition while you research different travel options: there are plenty of ways you can travel cheaply, including hostels, Airbnb and couch-surfing websites.

And remember – don't wait for the perfect time to take your trip. There is *never* a perfect time; tasks will always crop up that you feel you should prioritize over your dreams, but actually it's these wonderful experiences and memories that really matter in life. So go for it – explore, experience and enjoy!

My dream trip record sheet

Planning

Destination:

_____

Possible date for trip:

_____

Reasons I want to go there:

_____

_____

_____

Budget plans:

_____

_____

_____

Transport plans:

_____

_____

_____

Travelling companions:

_____

_____

_____

Trip record

Top five things about the trip:

1._____

2._____

3._____

4._____

5._____

Funniest moment:

_____

_____

Scariest moment:

_____

_____

Best view:

_____

_____

Quote of the trip:

_____

_____

Where I might go next:

_____

_____

Build your bucket list

There are always more adventures to plan, more places to see and more experiences to try out. Writing your own bucket list will motivate you and keep you inspired. It's fun to do, there are no wrong answers and you can include anything you like from big life-changing plans to smaller items you can tick off in an afternoon if you make the time.

In this book we've already thought about the things that make you happy, as well as your values and priorities, so take a look back at these lists – and the questionnaire overleaf – for some inspiration. You can also search online for bucket list templates and blogs to get you started. Once you've drawn up your list, pick your first ambition and go for it... then rather than lying awake at night worrying about your to-do list, you can dream about your bucket list instead.

My bucket list questionnaire

Use these questions to get you thinking about what to include on your bucket list.

Places I'd like to go:

_____

_____

People I'd like to meet:

_____

_____

Skills I'd like to learn:

_____

_____

Wildlife I'd like to encounter:

_____

_____

Wonders I'd like to see:

_____

_____

Things my friends have done that I'd like to try:

_____

_____

Art/bands/plays I'd like to see:

_____

_____

Fitness goals:

_____

_____

Career goals:

_____

_____

Relationship goals:

_____

_____

Things I've wanted to do since I was a child:

_____

_____

Crazy things I'd like to do:

_____

_____

If money was no object, I would:

_____

_____

A LIFE
well-lived

An extraordinary life will bring you extraordinary memories, and this chapter shows you how to make the most of them. There are creative ideas for recording your happiest moments, and questionnaires to help you reflect on what you've learned and achieved. And – since *life's a journey, not a destination* – you won't be left high and dry feeling that your adventure is at an end. In the following pages, there are more ideas for ensuring that every day feels special and that you always have an adventure or two on the horizon.

Your journey journal

The best souvenirs from a trip are always memories, so don't forget to document your life experiences as you go – the small changes as well as the bigger adventures. If you haven't already got a journal, it's probably time to get one now! You don't need to write down everything you've done each day, just use it as a tool to keep a note of your thoughts whenever you like.

There are so many different types you can choose from, including those with prompts to help you reflect, but there's no need to spend big. You can easily pick a simple notebook and write down whatever you need. There are lots of other ways to record your experiences too (see pages 138–139), but journals are great for scribbling down ideas and making lists, and they're a safe place to share your feelings.

Every day

is a

JOURNEY

MEMENTOES

It's so rewarding to celebrate your successes and relive your favourite moments by keeping a record of your adventures. How you choose to do it is up to you – it's a great chance for you to get creative – but you could start with one of the following ideas:

`Pin it`

Put up a pinboard and decorate it with photos, tickets and other keepsakes from your activities. Add quotes or words that sum up your achievements too.

`Take a picture`

Document your extraordinary days with photos. Make sure each picture is a memory-jogger and either print to display, share on social media or make a collage for your desktop.

`Go figure(s)`

If numbers are your thing, get technical and record your achievements as stats. There are dozens of life-logging apps to help you track everything from your exercise achievements to your travel destinations. You'll soon have charts aplenty to show how far you've come.

Build a bullet journal

Bullet-journaling is a creative way of organizing your plans and recording your experiences in thoughtfully designed pages. Check online for pointers to get started.

Get painting... or drawing... or...

If you love art, why not make a visual record of your adventures? You could draw a cartoon to capture your favourite moments from the week or create a poster to record your milestones.

... get writing

Don't forget that journal entries can be creative too. You can sum up your week in a poem, or even write events up as a newspaper report or short story.

A line a day

Write a sentence a day – every day – to sum up your experiences. This really makes you think about your memorable moments and is fun to look back on.

Get blogging or vlogging

>>>———————➤

Starting a blog or vlog (video log) to record your experiences can be really rewarding, especially if you're on a bit of a mission and have a life goal in mind. When you've found your niche and you blog about your passion, you'll attract followers who have the same interests, and a good blog can become a positive place to share knowledge, experiences, enthusiasm and encouragement.

It's super-easy to start a blog and there is – of course! – plenty of advice online about how to do it. Once you're up and running, knowing that you're due to post something will focus your mind and inspire you to make the effort to keep up with your challenges and your followers!

Chill out and CHECK IN

Hopefully you've had a chance to try out plenty of the suggestions in this book: you've worked out what makes you happy, added fun to each and every day, and have started enjoying some bigger adventures too. But now you're living your extraordinary life, don't forget to find time to reflect on everything you've achieved.

Check in on your progress regularly – and make your "review" something to look forward to. Settle down in your favourite comfy corner with an indulgent treat, and look back through your journal and this book. Think about your achievements and note down whatever you'd like to work on next. (Remember that taking time out to reflect can be as beneficial for the mind as exercise is for the body, so these sessions are important.)

Dream big, work hard and CELEBRATE EVERY SUNRISE

My best moments

These pages will help you celebrate your latest, and greatest, achievements.

My happiest moment:

_____
_____
_____
_____

The things I'm most grateful for:

_____
_____
_____
_____

My biggest achievement:

_____
_____
_____
_____

How this made me feel:

_____
_____
_____
_____

The steps I took toward my dreams:

_____

_____

_____

_____

What I've learned:

_____

_____

_____

_____

Compliments and kindnesses

Received:

_____

_____

_____

_____

Given:

_____

_____

_____

_____

Adventure is worthwhile in itself.

Amelia Earhart

Goal check-in

Every so often it's useful to look back at the goals you set yourself and see how you're getting on. It will help to rekindle your passions or show you where new plans or strategies could be put into place. Fill out this table when you're ready to revisit your goals and compare it to the one you completed on pages 56–57.

AREA	What goal did you set yourself?	What steps have you taken?
Work		
Physical health		
Emotional well-being		
Family		
Home		
Hobbies		
Relationships		
Causes that matter to me		
Creative		
Any others (e.g. spiritual)		

How do you feel about this area of your life now? ☺ / 😐 / ☹	What would you like to do next?

Positivity place

This page is a little reminder of the resources you have to help you on your way to greatness. Revisit this list whenever you need to remember what makes your life – and you – wonderful. These are all powerful positives to have on your side.

My strengths (your top three positive qualities):

_____

_____

_____

My skills (from sketching to negotiating to locating missing socks):

_____

_____

_____

My team (the friends and loved ones who brighten my day):

_____

_____

_____

My top three de-stressors (the activities that immediately calm you):

1._____

2._____

3._____

My personal statement (see page 29):

Twelve ways to transform your day

1. Breathe properly (see page 8)

2. Be present – notice the details in your surroundings

3. Eat well and drink plenty of water

4. Laugh... a lot

5. Go outside and experience the weather

6. Connect with someone

7. Have two mini-sessions of "me time": one to practise de-stressing...

8. ... and one to do something you love

9. Be grateful

10. Carry out an act of kindness

11. Listen to music, dance and/or sing

12. Write or reflect on your day

Small
changes
make a big
difference

Each day is a journey, and the journey itself is home.

Matsuo Bashō

Keep challenging yourself

There are always more challenges to take on and more experiences to be had, so if you've achieved a lifelong dream, don't feel that the adventure is ending. Make sure that you take time to enjoy your achievement, but keep your eyes open for new opportunities or directions you'd like to explore.

Remember, though, that happiness is all about taking pleasure in your day-to-day activities, not something to be put off until you complete another challenge, so if you suddenly find your life feeling a little empty or without direction, focus back on the little things. Remind yourself of the things you're grateful for every day, enjoy some mindful moments, and your next big challenge will be waiting round the corner.

Conclusion

Well, you've reached the end of the book but not – of course – the end of your adventure. I hope that your journey is just beginning as you fall in love again with your extraordinary life. Don't forget to embrace the good bits, learn from the bad bits and celebrate all the brilliant moments in between.

Life's certainly a journey that sweeps us along, but remember that *you* get to choose the direction and to set the pace. So pick an interesting route, look forward to a detour or two and set out with optimism and excitement in your heart. Most importantly, though, cherish the memories you make with your fellow travellers along the way.

Enjoy your trip!

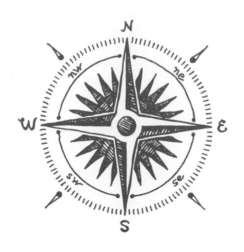

*Focus on the journey,
not the destination. Joy is
found not in finishing an
activity but in doing it.*

GREG ANDERSON

If you're interested in finding out more about our books, find us on Facebook at **Summersdale Publishers** and follow us on Twitter at **@Summersdale**.

www.summersdale.com

Image credits